ILLUSTRATED SOFTBALL RULES

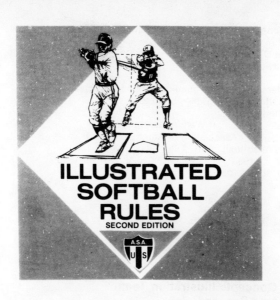

ILLUSTRATED SOFTBALL RULES

SECOND EDITION

by
Merle O. Butler
and
Johnny W. Welton, Ed.D.

Mike Wood, Artist

Contemporary Books, Inc.
Chicago

Library of Congress Cataloging in Publication Data

Butler, Merle O.
  Illustrated softball rules.

  Cross-referenced to the Amateur Softball Association
of America Official playing rules of softball.
  Includes index.
  1. Softball—Rules.   I. Welton, Johnnie W.
II. Amateur Softball Association of America. Official
playing rules of softball.   III. Title.
GV881.2.B87   1983   796.357'8'02022   83-1836
ISBN 0-8092-5521-9 (pbk.)

Books by Concepts Illustration Team
  Illustrated Soccer Rules
  Illustrated Softball Rules

Published by Contemporary Books, Inc.
180 North Michigan Avenue, Chicago, Illinois 60601
Manufactured in the United States of America
Library of Congress Catalog Card Number: 83-1836
International Standard Book Number: 0-8092-5521-9

Published simultaneously in Canada by
Beaverbooks, Ltd.
150 Lesmill Road
Don Mills, Ontario M3B 2T5   Canada

Softball

D.E. PORTER
Executive Director

SOFTBALL'S PHENOMENAL GROWTH CAN BE ATTRIBUTED TO MANY
FACTORS, HOWEVER, ONE OF THE MOST IMPORTANT IS UNIFORM
PLAYING RULES.

SOME 30 MILLION-PLUS PARTICIPANTS COMPETE IN ORGANIZED
SOFTBALL AND THE LARGEST PERCENTAGE OF THE PARTICIPANTS
PLAY BY THE A.S.A. PLAYING RULES.

AS SOFTBALL GROWS AND BECOMES MORE ORGANIZED AND COMPET-
ITIVE ... THE NEED FOR PROFESSIONALLY TRAINED AND EXPER-
IENCED UMPIRES BECOMES MORE IMPORTANT.

TECHNICAL AIDS SUCH AS THE "ILLUSTRATED SOFTBALL RULES"
THAT HELP UMPIRES TO BETTER UNDERSTAND AND ADMINISTER
THE RULES OF THE GAME ARE A MUST.

Don Porter

Don E. Porter
Executive Director

1933-1982

AMATEUR SOFTBALL ASSOCIATION OF AMERICA

NATIONAL ASA HEADQUARTERS and HALL OF FAME • 2801 N.E. 50th St. • Oklahoma City, Oklahoma 73111 • (405) 424-5266

CONTENTS

New Rules

**Concepts
Illustration
Team**   **FOREWORD**

Concepts Illustration Team (CIT) shares your interest and enthusiasm for the exciting game of softball. This book, **Illustrated Softball Rules,** is designed to increase your understanding of softball rules through illustrations that capture the speed of softball and the excitement of actual play. Each rule interpretation is presented in a clear and concise way, including information for the players, as well as the umpires, with cross-references to the Official Softball Rules. We hope this book increases your enjoyment of softball and improves your game on the field.

ILLUSTRATED SOFTBALL RULES

LEGEND

Players: What will happen

Umpires: What to do

Reference: Where to find it in the Official Rules of Softball

(SP ONLY): Plays following this notation apply to Slow Pitch only

(FP ONLY): Plays following this notation apply to Fast Pitch only
When there is no notation to (FP ONLY) or (SP ONLY), the interpretation is valid for both Fast and Slow Pitch.

NOTE: Rules referring to 16-inch Slow Pitch, Modified Fast Pitch, and Youth Softball are covered in *New Rules* section Only.

1983 OFFICIAL
SOFTBALL RULE CHANGES

as adopted by the Amateur Softball Association of America (A.S.A.A.)

RULE CHANGES, INTERPRETATIONS, AND CLARIFICATIONS EFFECTIVE JANUARY 1, 1983

The type of rule change is indicated in the following key.

Key to Divisions: (A) = All Divisions
(FP) = Fast Pitch
(SP) = Slow Pitch
(M) = Modified
(16") = Sixteen Inch

RULE CHANGES

Rule	Type	Description

Rule	Type	Description
1-28	A	A helmet may be worn by the batter, baserunner, catcher, or pitcher.
1-38	A	Removes catcher interference from "Interference" definition.
1-42	A	"Catcher Interference" is added here and redefined as "Catcher Obstruction."
1-51	A	Defines runner as "Batter-runner" or "Baserunner."

Rule	Type	Description

LEGAL   **ILLEGAL**

3–1   A   A legal bat must have a 1/4-inch safety knob on the handle end. Flare or cone grips are illegal.

ILLEGAL

3–1   A   The on-deck batter may only use an official softball bat or an approved warm-up bat for loosening up. No bat attachments or lead pipes are legal.

3–2   SP   The RF-80 ball is now trademarked with yellow/gold thread and must be used in all men's Slow Pitch and Co-Ed Slow Pitch championship play. Existing inventories of red-stitched RF-80 balls will be allowed in 1983 only.

3–8   FP   Catchers must wear throat protectors on the mask for all adult or youth Fast Pitch play. Youth catchers must wear body protectors.

3-10a (2)   A   Headgear is optional for female players. However, if one player wears a cap, visor, or headband, all other players choosing to wear headgear must wear the same type.

3–10c   A   The defensive pitcher may wear a helmet.

3–10e   A   No player may wear a cast made of plaster, metal, or other hard substance. A player may wear exposed metal only if it is covered by soft material and taped.

Rule	Type	Description
4–1d	A	Male rosters must include only male players and female rosters must include only female players. Co-ed rosters must include both males and females.
4–6a	A	All player substitutions must be reported to the umpires. Unannounced substitutes are ejected from the game when brought to the umpire's attention. All plays made by or on an illegal substitute are considered legal. If an illegal substitute violates the re-entry rule, the game is forfeited.
5–9	A	A manager or coach who insists on a second offensive conference in the same half-inning is ejected.
6–1	M	Defines the Modified Fast Pitch differences from regular fast pitching.
6–1b	16"	The pitcher must deliver the ball within 10 seconds after pausing.
6–3c	16"	The minimum height of the pitched ball is 6 feet (1.83 m) from the ground.
6–4	16"	After a pick-off attempt, the hesitation count does not start over.
6–4f	FP	Each pitch does not have to be consistent in motion.
6–6	FP	If an illegal pitch is called and the ball hits the batter, the batter is awarded first base and all runners advance one base.
7–2a	A	A game is not forfeited if a manager or captain fails to give the umpire a line-up before the start of the game. However, the line-up is still required.
7–11j	SP	Removes the foul-ball-third-strike rule from youth Slow Pitch.
8–6h	16"	Clarifies the lead-off rule in 16-inch Slow Pitch.
8–7k	A	The batter is out when a batted ball is hit a second time with a bat or when it hits the body of the batter outside of the batter's box.
8–8v	A	A runner is called out when he or she abandons a base and enters the team area or leaves the field.

| Rule | Type | Description |

10-1c FP   Body protectors are recommended for both male and female umpires in Fast Pitch.

12-9   A   All records of a forfeited game must be included in the official records except the pitcher's record.

Section 1

Rules 1, 2, 3, 4 and 5

**Definitions, the Playing Field, Equipment
Players and Substitutes, and the Game**

Players: When the ball is held in the hands or glove of a fielder the catch
is legal and the batter is out. At no time can the ball touch the ground or
another object (including an umpire) before a catch is legal. The ball
can be juggled, but the catch is not complete until firmly held in the
hand or hands of the fielder.

Umpires: Delay the call until you are sure the play has been completed.
Signal and call "Out." Runners tagging up can leave their bases when
the ball is first touched.

Reference: Rule 1, Sec. 12; Rule 7, Sec. 11c; Rule 1, Sec. 39.

Players: It is not considered a catch when a fielder, immediately after contact with the ball, collides with another player, a wall, or the ground and drops the ball. To complete the catch, the fielder must hold the ball long enough to prove he or she has complete control of it.

Umpires: Delay your call until you are sure the play has been completed. Signal and call "Out" or "Safe."

Reference: Rule 1, Sec. 12 and 39.

Players: When a fielder drops a ball he or she is attempting to throw, the catch is still considered valid.

Umpires: Delay your call until the play is completed. Be sure the requirements for the catch or the timing for the force-out have been met. Signal and call "Out."

Reference: Rule 1, Sec. 12 and 39.

Players: When the ball is held in the hands or glove of a fielder, even if it has touched another player, the catch is legal and the batter is out. At no time can the ball touch the ground or another object (including an umpire) before a catch is legal.

Umpires: Delay your call until you are sure the play has been completed. Signal and call "Out." Remember, a runner tagging up can leave the base when the ball is first touched by a fielder even if caught by another fielder.

Reference: Rule 1, Sec. 12; Rule 7, Sec. 11c; Rule 1, Sec. 39.

Players: A batted ball that settles on home plate is considered a fair ball.
Umpires: Signal "Fair Ball." No verbal call is made.
Reference: Rule 1, Sec. 21; Rule 7, Sec. 8a.

(A)

(B)

Players: A foul tip is a batted ball which goes directly from the bat, not higher than the batter's head, to the catcher's hands and is legally caught by the catcher (A). If the ball first touches anything other than the hand or glove of the catcher, it is a foul ball (B). All foul tips are called strikes.

Umpires: Signal and call "Foul Tip — Strike" or signal and call "Foul Ball."

Reference: Rule 1, Sec. 27.

Players: An infield fly is a live ball situation. The runners may advance at their own risk. If the fly is caught, the runners must tag up as with any other caught fly ball. An infield fly is a fair ball (not including a line drive nor an attempted bunt) which can be caught by an infielder with ordinary effort when first and second, or first, second, and third bases are occupied with less than two outs.

Umpires: Signal and call "Infield Fly" if fair. Then signal and call "Batter Out." Be alert for subsequent plays. Signal and call "Time" only when it is apparent that no further play will be made.

Reference: Rule 1, Sec. 35; Rule 9, Sec. 2c; Rule 7, Sec. 11d.

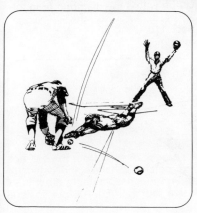

Players: An infield fly must be a fair ball for the batter to be called out. When no player touches the fly ball and it rolls into foul territory, it is a foul ball.

Umpires: When the ball reaches its highest point, signal and call "Infield Fly" if fair. Determine fair or foul ball as for any other batted ball. Signal and call "Foul Ball" or signal "Fair Ball." If the ball is caught or the ball is fair, the batter is out.

Reference: Rule 1, Sec. 35; Rule 7, Sec. 11d; Rule 10, Sec. 7e, 7f, and 7n.

(A)

Players: An infield fly is a fair fly ball (A), not including a bunt (C) or line drive (B), which can be caught by an infielder with ordinary effort.
Umpires: Try to determine if the fly is an infield fly at the time the ball reaches its highest point. Signal and call "Infield Fly" if fair. Then signal and call "Batter Out." An infielder need not attempt the play even though the ball could have been caught. Usually the infielder will have time to go to the ball and face home plate during the attempt. After calling the infield fly, the attempt may be within the diamond or in the outfield by an infielder or outfielder.
Reference: Rule 1, Sec. 35; Rule 7, Sec. 11d.

(B)

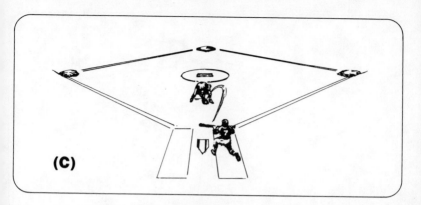

Players: The batter must stand within the lines of the batter's box when striking the ball. A batter is considered out of the box when a foot is on the ground entirely outside the lines, or when a foot touches home plate at the time the bat contacts the ball. When this occurs, the ball is illegally batted whether it is fair or foul. If the batter swings and misses, only a strike is called.

Umpires: When a batter illegally bats a ball, signal and call "Time" — illegally batted ball. The ball is dead immediately, all runners must return to the last base touched, and the batter is called out.

Reference: Rule 1, Sec. 30 and 7.

Players: A fielder may not tag a runner with the glove hand while holding the ball in the other hand. The runner must be tagged with the hand holding the ball. NOTE: If the runner is tagged by the glove *with the ball inside*, then the runner would be called out.

Umpires: Signal and call "Safe" if the runner was not tagged with the ball.

Reference: Rule 1, Sec. 38.

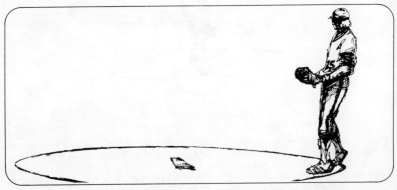

Players: The line drawn around the pitcher's plate is considered inside the circle.

Umpires: A player standing on the line is considered inside the circle.

Reference: Rule 2, Sec. 4.

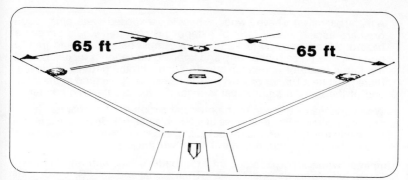

Players: The official diamond has 60-foot (1829 cm) base lines with pitching distances as follows: Adult Fast Pitch: Male — 46 feet (1402 cm), Female — 40 feet (1219 cm). Youth Fast Pitch: Girls — 40 feet (1219 cm), Boys — 46 feet (1402 cm). Slow Pitch: Girls — 40 feet (1219 cm), Boys — 46 feet (1402 cm).

Exception: Adult Male Slow Pitch has 65-foot (19.81 m) base lines.

Umpires: Check the base lines and pitching distances prior to the start of the game.

Reference: Rule 2, Sec. 3.

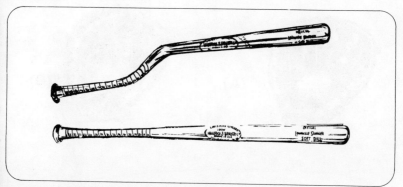

Players: The legal bat should be marked "Official Softball" and can be made of plastic, metal, bamboo, or wood. The bat should be no longer than 34 inches and no more than 2-1/4 inches in diameter at the largest point, and should not weigh more than 38 ounces. The bat must have a safety grip of cork, tape (not smooth plastic type), or composition material only which should be no less than 10 inches long and may not extend more than 15 inches from the small end of the bat.

A metal bat may not have a wooden handle or exposed rivets, pins, rough or sharp edges, or any form of exterior fastener that would present a hazard. All exposed surfaces of the bat must be smooth and free of burrs. A one-piece rubber grip and knob combination is illegal. Unless the bat is made of one-piece construction with the barrel end closed, there must be a rubber or vinyl plastic insert firmly secured at the large end of the bat. An angular bat is legal if it meets other requirements.

When changes are made to the physical structure of a legal bat, it becomes an altered bat. Examples of altering a bat include inserting material inside the bat, painting the bat, using excessive pine tar or tape on or above the safety grip, and sanding down the bat.

Umpires: When a player steps into the batter's box with an altered or illegal bat, signal and call "Time." Then signal and call "Batter Out." If the bat is altered, remove the player from the game.

Reference: Rule 3, Sec. 1; Rule 1, Sec. 1; Rule 7, Sec. 1c;

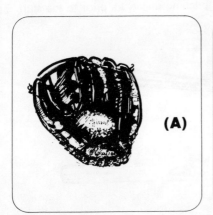 **(A)**

 **(B)**

Players: Gloves (A) may be worn by any player, but mitts (B) may be used only by the catcher and the first baseman. The pitcher's glove must be of one solid color other than white or grey. Multi-color gloves are acceptable for all other players. The batter is not out if the fielder making a play on him or her uses an illegal glove.

Umpires: If you see a fielder other than a first baseman or catcher using a mitt, have it removed. If the violation is not noticed until after an out is made with an illegal glove, the manager of the offended team has the option of having the batter bat again (assuming the same ball and strike count before the pitch hit) or accepting the result of the play. Signal and call "Time" and consult the team manager.

Reference: Rule 3, Sec. 6; Rule 7, Sec. 12.

Players: Shoes must be worn at all times. They may be made of canvas or leather uppers or similar material. The soles may be either smooth or have soft or hard rubber cleats. Shoes with metal spikes are legal if the spikes are not longer than 3/4-inch from the sole or heel of the shoe. Shoes with rounded metal spikes (golf, football, or track shoes) are illegal.

Umpires: If illegal shoes are noticed, signal and call "Time." Ask the player to change them. A player not removing illegal shoes could be removed from the game. Players not wearing shoes may not play.

Reference: Rule 3, Sec. 7.

6 in.

Players: All players on a team must wear uniforms alike in color, trim, and style. Ball caps must be alike and are mandatory for all male players and must be worn properly. Caps, visors, and headbands are optional for female players, but may not be mixed. If one of the above is worn, all other players choosing to wear headgear must wear the same type. Team players may wear undershirts of a uniform, solid in color (it may be white). It is not mandatory that all team players wear an undershirt if one player wears one, but those that are worn must be alike. No player may wear ragged, frayed, or slit sleeves on exposed undershirts. A number of contrasting color, at least 6 inches high, must be worn on the back of all uniform shirts. No players on the same team may wear identical numbers.

Umpires: Request the player to correct the improper clothing. Players can be removed from the game for not conforming to the rules.

Reference: Rule 3, Sec. 10.

Players: Male team players must wear ball caps which are alike. The caps must be worn properly. Helmets are permissible for batters, runners, pitchers and catchers. Helmets may not be worn by any defensive player except the catcher or pitcher unless for medical purposes.

Umpires: If ball caps are not worn or are improperly worn, call "Time." Warn the player and the team manager. Players can be removed from the game for not conforming to the rules.

Reference: Rule 4, Sec. 10a.

LEGAL

ILLEGAL

Players: Team players may wear undershirts of a uniform solid color (it may be white). It is not mandatory that all team players wear an undershirt if one player wears one, but those that are worn, must be alike. No player may wear ragged, frayed, or slit sleeves on exposed undershirts.

Umpires: If it is noticed that players of the same team have different colored undershirts or that any player has a ragged undershirt, notify the manager to correct the situation. Players can be removed from the game for not conforming to the rules.

Reference: Rule 3, Sec. 10b.

OFFICIAL BATTING ORDER

Tournament _____

Location _____ _____ Date _____

TEAM NAME _____

	ORIGINAL	POS.	Jersey Number
1.	JONES	CF	16
2.	SMITH	SS	22
3.	BROWN	1B	8
4.	WELTON	DH	7
5.	HARRIS	LF	19
6.	ROBERTS	RF	11
7.	MAYHOOD	C	1
8.	DOWLING	3B	6
9.	WOLFE	2B	9
10.	SMALL	P	39

Players: (FP ONLY) A Designated Hitter (DH) is allowed in the Fast Pitch game only. The DH must be indicated on the line-up card at the beginning of the game. The DH must remain in the same position in the batting order the entire game. The team using a DH must start and finish with ten players. A DH may never play defense. A DH may not re-enter the game after a substitution has been made for him or her with a batter or runner. The substitute remains in the game as the DH. The substitute must be a player who has not yet been in the game.

Umpires: Indicate the DH and all substitutes on your line-up cards. When no cards are available, consult the scorekeeper if questioned on DH participation and substitutions. If an illegal substitution occurs before the first pitch, correct the situation and resume play with no penalty. If the illegal participation occurs and is noticed at any time after the first pitch has been thrown, declare the game forfeited.

Reference: Rule 4, Sec. 3.

A Slow Pitch team consists of ten players. Teams must have ten players to start or continue play.

The Designated Hitter (DH) rule does not apply to Slow Pitch.

Umpires: If it is noticed after the game has begun that a team does not have ten players, the game is forfeited.

Reference: Rule 4, Sec. 1, 2 and 5.

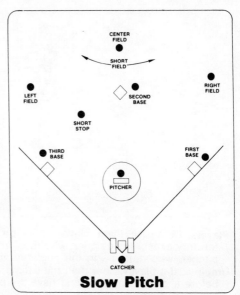

Slow Pitch

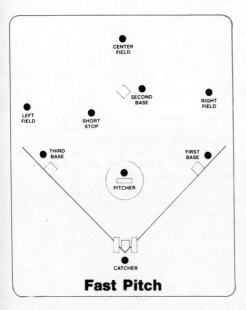

Fast Pitch

A Fast Pitch team consists of nine players. Teams must have nine players to start or continue play.

A Designated Hitter (DH) is allowed in the Fast Pitch game. If a team using a DH starts with ten players, it must finish with ten players. If a DH is not in the starting line-up, he or she cannot be added later in the game.

Umpires: If it is noticed after the game has begun that a team does not have nine players (ten with the DH), the game is forfeited.

Reference: Rule 4, Sec. 1, 2 and 5.

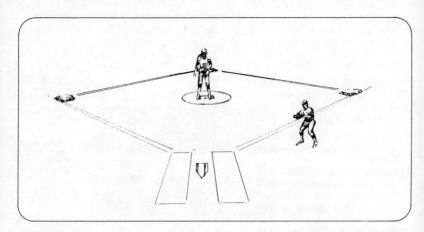

Players: Defensive team players may be stationed anywhere on fair territory except the catcher, who must be in the catcher's box, and the pitcher, who must be in the pitching circle.

Umpires: If a player other than the catcher is positioned in foul territory before a pitch, stop play and have the player move between the two fair lines. If player refuses to move, eject the offender.

Reference: Rule 4, Sec. 2.

	ORIGINAL	POS.	Jersey Number
1.	JONES	CF	16
2.	SMITH	SS	22
3.	BROWN	1B	8
4.	WELTON *	SF	7
5.	(HARRIS)	LF	19
	CARTER	LF	13
6.	ROBERTS	RF	11
7.	MAYHOOD	C	1
8.	DOWLING	3B	6
9.	WOLF	2B	25
10.	SMALL	P	39

*SF — Slow pitch for short fielder

Players: (FP ONLY) Any of the starting players except a Designated Hitter may leave and re-enter the game once, provided the player occupies the same batting position in the line-up.

A starting player can be replaced at bat and in the field.

Once a substitute is replaced by the starting player, the substitute may not re-enter the game.

Umpires: Violation of the re-entry rule results in the use of an ineligible player. Declare a forfeit when the violation is brought to your attention by the offended team. It is handled as a protest, which can be made anytime during the game. The protest need not be made before the next pitch as described in Rule 11, Sec. 4.

Reference: Rule 4, Sec. 4 and Rule 11, Sec. 7c.

	1	2	3	4	5	6	7	T
VISITOR	2	1	0	0	0			3
HOME	0	2	2	0	X			4

	1	2	3	4	5	6	7	T
VISITOR	2	1	0	1	0			4
HOME	0	0	2	0	1			3

A regulation game may be called after 4-1/2 innings with the home team ahead or after a full 5 innings with the visitors ahead. The umpire is empowered to suspend play at any time because of darkness, rain, fire, panic, or any other cause which puts the patrons or players in peril.

	1	2	3	4	5	6	7	T
VISITOR	1	1	0	2	0	1	0	5
HOME	0	2	3	0	0	2	X	7

A regulation game is 7 innings unless the home team scores more runs in 6 innings than the visitors score in 7 innings.

	1	2	3	4	5	6	7	8	9	10	T
VISITOR	1	1	0	3	0	0	0	0			5
HOME	0	2	0	2	1	0	0	0			5

A regulation tie game is declared if the score is equal when the game is called at the end of 5 or more completed innings, or if the team second at bat has equaled the score of the first team at bat in the incomplete inning.

Games that are not considered regulation or regulation tie games must be replayed from the beginning. Original line-ups may be changed when the game is replayed.

Reference: Rule 5, Sec. 4, 3a–d.

A RUN WILL NOT SCORE if the third out of the inning is the result of:

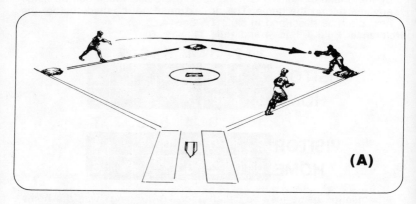

(A)

(A) The batter being put out before legally touching first base.
Umpires: Following the third out indicate that no runs score.
Reference: Rule 5, Sec. 6a.

(B)

(B) A runner being forced out by the batter-runner.
Umpires: Following the third out, indicate that no runs score.
Reference: Rule 5, Sec. 6b.

(C)

(C) A runner leaving a base (FP) before the pitcher releases the ball or (SP) before the pitched ball reaches home plate or is batted.
Umpires: Signal and call "Time." Then signal and call "Runner Out" for leaving too soon. Following the third out, indicate that no runs score.
Reference: Rule 5, Sec. 6c; Rule 8, Sec. 8t (FP) and 8u (SP).

(D)

(D) A preceding runner being called out.
Umpires: If a preceding runner is called out on an appeal, no succeeding runner may score. Following the third out, indicate that no runs score.
Reference: Rule 5, Sec. 7.

23

Players: There may be only one charged offensive conference between the manager or other team representative and the batter or baserunner in an inning.

Umpires: More than one conference per inning is not allowed. If a player or manager refuses to comply with your order to play ball, remove the offender.

Reference: Rule 5, Sec. 9.

Players: If an appeal play is made on the runner after a preceding runner crosses home plate, the run counts. If the preceding runner has not crossed home plate at the time of the appeal, no runs will score.

Umpires: Determine the position of the preceding runner at the time the appeal play is made on the trailing runner. Signal and call either "Out" or "Safe" for the preceding runner.

Reference: Rule 5, Sec. 6.

Players: If the third out of the inning is the batter-runner who misses first base, no runs will score.

or

Players: If a batter hits a home run, misses first base, and the proper appeal is made, the batter-runner is out. No runs will score if the batter-runner is the third out of the inning.

Umpires: Each base must be touched and in proper order. If the defensive team makes the proper appeal and the batter-runner is called out for missing first base, no runs will score.

Reference: Rule 5, Sec. 5 and 6a.

Players: When the batter hits a home run but misses a base, the batter-runner is out if the proper appeal is made.

Umpires: If properly appealed, signal and call "Batter-Runner Out." All preceding runners would score if they crossed home plate before the appeal was made, unless the base missed was first base for the third out.

Reference: Rule 5, Sec. 5 and 7; Rule 8, Sec. 8g.

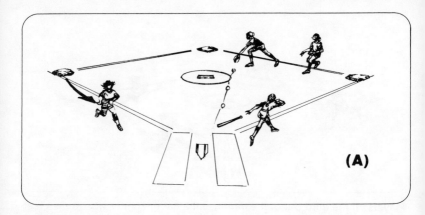

(A)

Players: If a third out of an inning is a runner (A) who is forced out by the batter-runner, no runs will score. It does not matter if a third base runner crosses home plate before the force-out (B) — the run does not count.

Umpires: Signal and call "Out" for both runners. Notify the scorekeeper that the run does not count.

Reference: Rule 5, Sec. 6b.

(B)

Players: If the batter hits a home run but the third base runner misses home plate, the runner is out if the proper appeal is made. No succeeding runs will score if the third base runner is the third out of the inning. It does not matter if all succeeding runners touch the bases in proper order — no runs will score.

Umpires: If the proper appeal is made on the third base runner who missed home plate, signal and call "Runner Out." No runs will score since the third out was a force-out.

Reference: Rule 5, Sec. 6b; Rule 8, Sec. 1f and g.

Section 2
Rule 6
(Fast & Slow Pitch)

Pitching Regulations

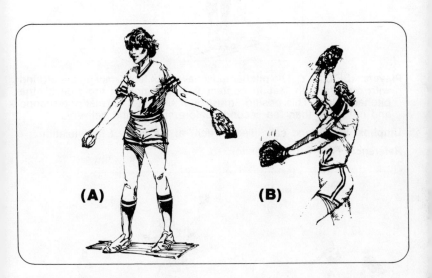

(A)   **(B)**

Players: (FP ONLY) Before starting the delivery, the pitcher must comply with the following:

(A) Both feet must be on the ground and in contact with (but not off the side of) the pitcher's plate. The shoulders must be in line with first and third bases and the ball must be held in one hand. While in this position, the pitcher must take the signal from the catcher.

(B) After receiving the catcher's signal, the ball must be held in both hands for not less than one second and not more than ten seconds before the release.

Umpires: Signal and call "Illegal Pitch" at the time of the violation.

Reference: Rule 6 (FP), Sec. 1a and b.

Players: (SP ONLY) The pitcher must have both feet firmly on the ground with one or both feet in contact with, but not off the side of, the pitcher's plate. This position must be maintained at least one second and not more than ten seconds before starting the delivery.

Umpires: Signal and call "Illegal Pitch" at the time of the violation.

Reference: Rule 6 (SP), Section 1b.

Players: (FP ONLY) The pitcher may not assume a pitching position on or near the pitching plate without having the ball in his or her possession.

Umpires: Signal and call "Illegal Pitch" and enforce the penalty.

Reference: Rule 6 (FP), Sec. 1e.

LEGAL

LEGAL

Players: (FP ONLY) During the delivery, the pitcher may not take more than one step, which must be forward toward the batter and made simultaneously with the release of the ball. The pivot foot must remain in contact with the pitching plate until the other foot (with which the pitcher steps forward) has touched the ground.

Umpires: It is legal for the pitcher to drag the foot during the step, as long as contact is maintained with the ground. The pitcher may use the pitching plate to push off on the step. When both feet are in the air at the same time, it is considered a hop and is illegal. Immediately signal and call "Illegal Pitch" at the time of the violation. Signal "Delayed Dead Ball."

Reference: Rule 6 (FP), Sec. 2.

LEGAL

ILLEGAL

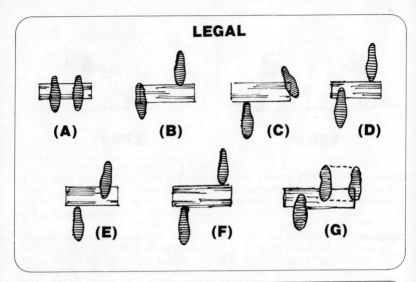

LEGAL

(A) **(B)** **(C)** **(D)**

(E) **(F)** **(G)**

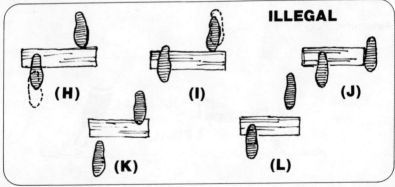

ILLEGAL

(H) **(I)** **(J)**

(K) **(L)**

Players: (FP ONLY) The pitcher must have both feet firmly on the ground and in contact with the pitching plate and not off to the side of the plate during the delivery (A–F). It is legal when a foot slides on the pitching plate (G) . It is illegal when a foot slides behind or in front of the pitching plate before the delivery (H and I). It is illegal when a foot is off to the side of the pitching plate or is not touching the plate (J–L).

Umpires: Either the plate umpire or the field umpire may signal and call "Illegal Pitch." Make the call loud enough for the catcher and batter or fielder to hear. Signal "Delayed Dead Ball."

Reference: Rule 6 (FP), Sec. 1 and 2 NOTE.

Players: (FP ONLY) If the pitcher on the pitching plate separates both hands, he or she must begin the pitch. If the pitcher separates both hands but does nothing, throws to a base from the plate, or brings both hands together again, it is considered an illegal pitch. NOTE: If the pitcher is not going to deliver a pitch, he or she must step back off the plate with both feet.

Umpires: Immediately signal and call "Illegal Pitch." If the pitcher throws to a base on an appeal play when one or both feet are in contact with the plate, immediately signal and call "Illegal Pitch," cancel the appeal, and enforce the penalty.

Reference: Rule 6 (FP), Sec. 2.

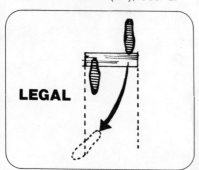
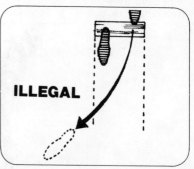

Players: (FP ONLY) During the delivery, the pitcher may not take more than one step, which must be forward toward the batter within the 24-inch length of the pitching plate. The step forward must be made simultaneously with the release of the ball. NOTE: It is not considered a step when the pitcher slides a foot across the pitching plate, provided that contact is maintained with the pitching plate.

Umpires: If the foot is inside or on the imaginary lines extending outward from the 24-inch length of the pitching plate, the step is legal. If the foot is entirely outside the imaginary lines, the step is illegal. Immediately signal and call "Illegal Pitch." Signal "Delayed Dead Ball."

Reference: Rule 6 (FP), Sec. 2.

Players: (FP ONLY) A pitcher's delivery must be a continuous motion. A pitcher, holding the ball in both hands in the pitching position, may not remove one hand from the ball, take a backward and forward swing, and return the ball to both hands in front of the body.

Umpires: Immediately signal and call "Illegal Pitch." Make the appropriate penalty awards.

Reference: Rule 6 (FP), Sec. 4b.

Players: (FP ONLY) A ball that accidentally falls from the pitcher's hand during delivery is considered a live ball and runners may advance. If the ball slips, hits the side of the pitcher's legs, and rolls toward the batter, during the delivery it would be considered a legal pitch.

Umpires: In both situations, the ball is in play. Allow all play to continue with runners advancing at their own risk.

Reference: Rule 6 (FP), Sec. 11; Rule 9, Sec. 2ad.

Players: (FP ONLY) A pitcher may drop his or her arm to the side and to the rear to begin the delivery (A). The hand must be below the hip and the wrist must not be farther out from the body than the elbow (B). The release of the ball and the follow-through of the hand and wrist must be forward past the straight line of the body (B and C). The pitcher may not continue to wind up after taking the forward step and simultaneously releasing the ball (D).

Umpires: Immediately call "Illegal Pitch" and signal "Delayed Dead Ball" for any violation of the pitching rules. Make the call loud enough for the batter and catcher to hear. Signal "Delayed Dead Ball."

Reference: Rule 6 (FP), Sec. 3 and 4.

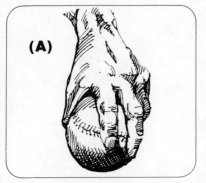

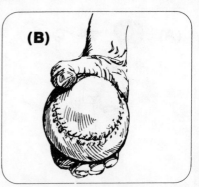

Players: (SP ONLY) The ball must be delivered in an underhand motion and released at a moderate speed. The hand must be below the hip. The pitcher can release the ball with his or her palm on top (A) or under (B) the ball.

Umpires: Observe the release in relationship to the body. Judging the speed of the pitch is entirely up to the umpire.

Reference: Rule 6 (SP), Sec. 3a and b.

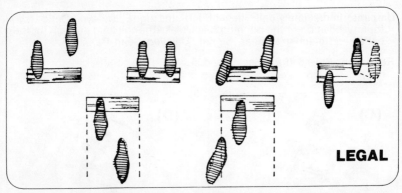

LEGAL

Players: (SP ONLY) The pitcher must take a position with both feet firmly on the ground and with one or both feet in contact with, but not off to the side of, the pitching plate. If a step is taken, it must be forward toward the batter, within the length of the pitching plate, and made simultaneously with the release of the ball.

Umpires: Immediately signal and call "Illegal Pitch" at the time of the violation. Signal "Delayed Dead Ball."

Reference: Rule 6 (SP), Sec. 1 and 2.

LEGAL **LEGAL** **ILLEGAL**

Players: (SP ONLY) The pitcher must have both feet firmly on the ground and one or both feet in contact with the pitching plate and not off to the side of the plate during the delivery. A step does not have to be made when releasing the ball, but if it is, it must be forward and within the 24-inch length of the pitching plate.

Umpires: Immediately signal and call "Illegal Pitch" at the time of the violation. Signal "Delayed Dead Ball." This will allow the batter time to decide whether to swing at the pitch or not. If the batter does not swing, the illegal pitch stands, the ball is dead, and the batter is awarded a ball.

Reference: Rule 6 (SP), Sec. 1 and 2.

ILLEGAL

Players: (SP ONLY) When a pitcher throws a flat excessive speed pitch, it is considered an illegal pitch.

Umpires: Immediately signal and call "Illegal Pitch" and warn the pitcher. If the pitcher throws a similar pitch after the warning, remove the pitcher from the pitching position for the remainder of the game. The player *may* play another position on defense.

Reference: Rule 6 (SP), Sec. 3a.

LEGAL

LEGAL

Players: (SP ONLY) A legal delivery is a ball which is delivered to the batter with an underhand motion and released at a moderate speed. The pitcher may use any wind-up desired provided the wind-up is a continuous motion and delivered on the first forward swing of the pitching arm past the hip. The pitcher may not continue winding up after releasing the ball.

Umpires: Immediately signal and call "Illegal Pitch" at the time of the violation. Signal "Delayed Dead Ball."

Reference: Rule 6 (SP), Sec. 4a–f.

LEGAL

ILLEGAL

Players: (FP ONLY) A ball that accidentally falls from the pitcher's hand during the delivery is considered a live ball and runners may advance. (SP ONLY) A ball that accidentally falls from the pitcher's hand during the delivery will be declared a no pitch.

Umpires: (FP ONLY) The ball remains in play. Allow all play to continue with runners advancing at their own risk. If the pitch is delivered, it will be called as it crosses the area near the home plate. (SP ONLY) The ball is dead. Signal and call "Time — No Pitch."

Reference: Rule 6 (FP), Sec. 11; Rule 6 (SP), Sec. 9e.

Players: When a fielder, other than the catcher, picks up a foul ball or wild pitch and throws to another fielder with no runners on base, no violation occurs.

Umpires: Wait for the pitcher to receive the ball and put it into play.

Reference: Rule 6, Sec. 3e.

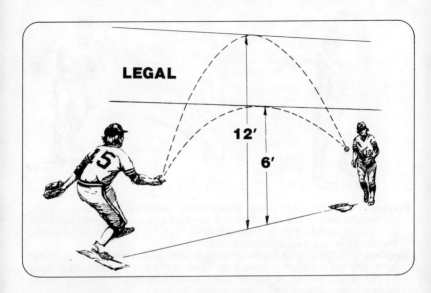

Players: (SP ONLY) The pitch must be delivered with a perceptible arc of at least 6 feet (1.83 m) from the ground. The pitched ball must not reach a height of more than 12 feet (3.66 m) at its highest point from the ground.

Umpires: Signal and call "Illegal Pitch" at the time of the violation.

Reference: Rule 6 (SP), Sec. 3.

(A)

Players: The catcher must return the ball directly to the pitcher after each pitch except after a batter strikes out or is tagged out by the catcher. (FP ONLY) This does not apply when a batter becomes a batter-runner or when there are runners on base.

Umpires: (FP) The catcher need not return the ball to the pitcher when there are runners on base (A) or when the batter becomes a batter-runner (B). (SP) The catcher must return the ball to the pitcher when there are runners on base (A) and the batter is not out. If there is a violation, award an additional ball to the batter.

Reference: Rule 6 (FP and SP), Sec. 3e.

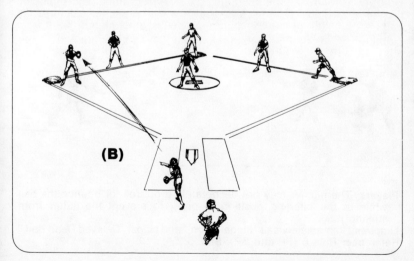

(B)

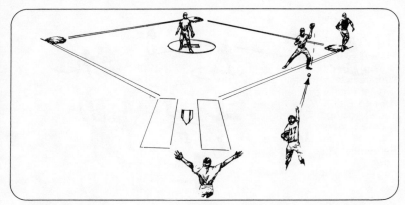

Players: (SP ONLY) A foul ball retrieved by the catcher may not be thrown to first base with a runner or runners on base. NOTE: In Slow Pitch, the pitched ball must be returned directly to the pitcher, even with runners on base.

Umpires: Award a ball to the batter. If the count was three balls before the pitch, award the batter first base.

Reference: Rule 6 (SP), Sec. 3e.

Players: The pitcher may not deliberately drop, roll, or bounce the ball while in the pitching position in order to prevent the batter from striking it.

Umpires: Immediately call "Illegal Pitch," and signal "Delayed Dead Ball."

Reference: Rule 6 (FP and SP), Sec. 5.

Players: A pitcher may not apply resin directly on the ball.

Umpires: Immediately call the "Illegal Pitch," and signal "Delayed Dead Ball." Warn the pitcher of the violation. Continued usage could warrant removal of the pitcher from the game.

Reference: Rule 6 (FP and SP, Sec. 6.

ILLEGAL → RESIN BAG

LEGAL ↓

Players: Under the control of the umpire, powdered resin may be used to dry the hands. The resin must be on the ground. It may not be in a back pocket, in a glove, or in any other location.

Umpires: Warn the player of the violation. Signal and call "Illegal Pitch" if a pitcher violates the rule. Continued violation could be cause to remove the player from the game.

Reference: Rule 6 (FP and SP), Sec. 6.

Players: Sweatbands, bracelets, or similar items may not be worn on the pitching arm. It is legal to wear sweatbands and batting gloves on the glove hand or arm.

Umpires: When it is noticed that a pitcher is wearing a sweatband on the pitching arm, ask him or her to remove it. If it is not removed, an illegal pitch will be called for each pitch thrown. Continued usage could warrant removal of the pitcher from the game.

Reference: Rule 6 (FP and SP), Sec. 6.

Players: At the beginning of each half-inning or when a pitcher relieves another, only five (5) pitches may be thrown to the catcher or another teammate.

Umpires: For each warm-up pitch in excess of five, the batter will be awarded a ball. The umpire should indicate the number of pitches to the catcher to prevent this from happening.

Reference: Rule 6 (FP and SP), Sec. 7.

ILLEGAL

Players: A pitcher may not throw to a base while a foot is in contact with the pitching plate. If the throw is made during an appeal play, the appeal is canceled. Stepping forward or sideways off the pitching plate constitutes an illegal pitch.

Umpires: Immediately call "Illegal Pitch," and signal "Delayed Dead Ball." The ball is dead. Make the appropriate awards.

Reference: Rule 6 (FP and SP), Sec. 8.

Players: It is an illegal pitch when a fielder takes up a position in the batter's line of vision or, with deliberate unsportsmanlike intent, distracts the batter. A pitch does not have to be released.

Umpires: Immediately signal and call "Illegal Pitch." The ball is dead. Make the appropriate penalty awards.

Reference: Rule 6 (FP and SP), Sec. 8 NOTE.

Players: No player, manager, or coach may call "Time" or employ any other word or act while the ball is in play for the obvious purpose of trying to make the pitcher throw an illegal pitch.

Umpires: Signal and call "Time— No Pitch." Issue a warning to the offending team. If the same team repeats the act, the offender will be removed from the game.

Reference: Rule 6 (FP), Sec. 9e; Rule 6 (SP), Sec. 9f.

NO PITCH WILL BE CALLED

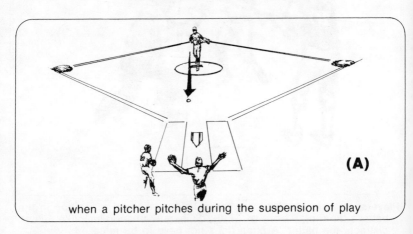

(A)

when a pitcher pitches during the suspension of play

Umpires: Signal and call "Time" and step away from the plate. The ball is dead and all subsequent action on that pitch is canceled.

Reference: Rule 6 (FP and SP), Sec. 9.

when a pitcher attempts a quick return before the batter is in position,

when a runner is called out for leaving a base too soon, or

when a pitcher pitches before a runner has retouched a base after a foul ball is called and the ball is dead.

Players: One conference is allowed between a team representative from the dugout and each and every pitcher in an inning. Any second charged conference will result in the removal of the pitcher from the pitching position for the remainder of the game. Should the team manager remove the pitcher prior to the second conference, no conference will be charged. Once the manager talks to the pitcher, it is considered a conference.

Umpires: Inform the manager or team representative after the first conference by raising an index finger and stating, "That's One Conference." Record conferences on your line-up card.

Reference: Rule 6, Sec. 10.

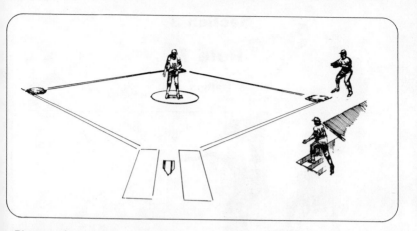

Players: A manager may shout to the players or the pitcher from the dugout and it is not considered a conference.
Umpires: Ignore the manager's comments. No conference is charged.
Reference: Rule 6, Sec. 10.

Players: When a team manager or representative from the dugout talks to another player on the field, who then goes to the pitcher before a pitch, it is considered a conference.
Umpires: Immediately inform the manager that one conference is charged. Any second conference in the same inning will result in the removal of the pitcher from the pitching position for the remainder of the game.
Reference: Rule 6, Sec. 10.

Section 3

Rule 7

Batting

Players: The batter must take his or her position within twenty (20) seconds after the umpire has called "Play Ball."

Umpires: Signal and call "Out" at the time of the violation.

Reference: Rule 7, Sec. 1e.

LEGAL

Players: The batter may not step across home plate to the other batter's box when the pitcher is on the pitching plate ready to pitch. NOTE: It is legal for the batter to step across the plate when the pitcher is in the 8-foot radius.

Umpires: Signal and call "Time." Then signal and call "Batter Out." The ball is dead. Runners may not advance.

Reference: Rule 7, Sec. 1b.

Players: When the batter is out of the batter's box and interferes with the catcher's fielding or throwing (whether intentional or not, with or without contact with the catcher), the umpire may call batter's interference.

Umpires: Signal "Delayed Dead Ball" and call "Batter's Interference." When there is no further play, signal and call "Time." If the runner attempting to advance is put out, the interference is ignored and the batter is warned. If the runner is not put out, all other runners must return to the last base touched at the time of the interference. Signal and call "Batter Out" unless the runner is attempting to advance to home plate with less than two outs. Signal and call "Out" for the runner from third base. The batter continues at bat.

Reference: Rule 7, Sec. 3 EFFECT (1) and (2).

Players: (FP ONLY) When a runner from third base attempts to reach home plate, interference is called when the batter interferes with the catcher attempting to make a play, provided the runner is not tagged out.

Umpires: Signal "Delayed Dead Ball" and call "Batter's Interference." If the runner safely reaches home with less than two outs, call "Runner Out." The batter continues at bat. With two outs, signal and call "Batter Out." The inning ends with no runs scoring. If the runner is tagged out, signal and call "Out" and ignore the interference.

Reference: Rule 7, Sec. 3 EFFECT (2).

Players: (FP ONLY) The batter may not hinder the catcher from fielding or throwing the ball by stepping out of the batter's box or intentionally hinder the catcher while standing within the batter's box.

Umpires: The plate umpire signals "Delayed Dead Ball" and calls "Batter's Interference (A)." The base umpire calls "Safe" or Out (B)." If the runner is out, the interference is ignored and the ball remains in play. If the runner attempting to steal is safe, signal and call "Time." Then signal and call "Batter Out." The ball is dead and all runners must return to the last base touched at the time of the interference.

Reference: Rule 7, Sec. 3 EFFECT (1).

Players: Members of the offensive team may not interfere (intentionally or unintentionally) with a fielder attempting to catch a foul fly ball. Contact with the fielder need not be made to be called interference. Offensive team members must move out of the fielder's way.

Umpires: Signal and call "Time" for interference. Then signal and call "Batter Out." The call is made whether or not the ball is caught. The ball is dead and all runners must return to the last base touched.

Reference: Rule 7, Sec. 4; Rule 9, Sec. 1h(5); Rule 1, Sec. 37.

Players: A bat which hits the ball a second time (fair or foul) is illegal (A), but a ball which hits a bat a second time may be legal (B). If the batter drops the bat and the ball rolls against the bat, the contact is ignored.

Umpires: A bat thrown or dropped with the intent to hinder the fielder is not only illegal, but dangerous to the players. You must watch the ball and keep an eye on the batter and the bat. If interference, signal and call "Time." Then signal and call "Batter Out." All runners must return to the last base touched.

Reference: Rule 7, Sec. 5 NOTE.

Players: The batter may not hit a fair ball with the bat a second time in fair territory. Contact made with the ball a second time in foul territory or entirely within the batter's box is a foul ball.

Umpires: Signal and call "Time" — illegally batted ball. Signal and call "Batter Out" if the batter hit a fair ball with the bat a second time in fair territory. The ball is dead and all runners must return to the last base touched.

Reference: Rule 7, Sec. 5.

STRIKE-TWO

Players: (SP ONLY) A strike is called by the umpire when a batter strikes at and misses and pitch, legal or illegal. A pitch which is not batted becomes a dead ball when it passes the batter. No runners may advance and no appeal can be made.

Umpires: Signal and call "Strike." The ball is dead. Ignore the illegal pitch if called.

Reference: Rule 7, Sec. 6b (SP ONLY); Rule 9, Sec. 1x.

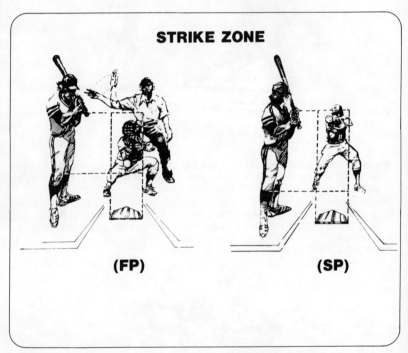

STRIKE ZONE

(FP)　　　　　**(SP)**

Players: A strike is called for each legally pitched ball that enters the strike zone before touching the ground or home plate, at which the batter does not swing. (FP) The strike zone is from the arm pits to the top of the knee. (SP) The strike zone is from the top of shoulder to the bottom of the knee. NOTE: In both games the strike zone is determined when the batter assumes his or her natural batting stance.

Umpires: Signal and call "Strike" followed by signal "One, Two or Three."

Reference: Rule 7, Sec. 6a; Rule 1, Sec. 53.

Players: (FP ONLY) A strike is called by the umpire when a batter strikes at and misses any legal pitch.
Umpires: Signal and call "Strike." The ball remains in play and runners may advance.
Reference: Rule 7, Sec. 6b (FP ONLY); Rule 9, Sec. 2aa.

Players: A batter who swings at a pitch and is hit by that pitch is not awarded a base. The pitch is a strike.
Umpires: Signal and call "Time." Then signal and call "Strike." The ball is dead and no runners may advance. If the batter hits the ball with a hand or an arm while attempting to swing and the ball rolls into fair territory, the ball is dead.
Reference: Rule 7, Sec. 6e; Rule 9, Sec. 1e.

Players: (SP ONLY) The batter is out when a third strike is called, including an uncaught foul ball that is hit after two strikes. EXCEPTION: In youth play, an uncaught foul ball is not a third strike.

Umpires: Signal and call "Strike Three." Then signal "Out."

Reference: Rule 7, Sec. 11j.

Players: A foul ball is called when a batter is hit by his or her own batted ball while in the batter's box.

Umpires: The ball is dead. Signal and call "Foul Ball." Observe the location of the batter's feet to determine where the batter is at the time of contact.

Reference: Rule 7, Sec. 6f; Rule 9, Sec. 1o.

Players: (FP ONLY) A strike is called by the umpire when a batter is hit by a pitch while the ball is in the strike zone. The ball is dead and all runners must return to the last base touched.

Umpires: Signal and call "Time." Then signal and call "Strike." If the pitch is in or has passed through the strike zone, it is a strike. The hands are not considered part of the bat.

Reference: Rule 7, Sec. 6g; Rule 9, sec. 1e (PLAY) and q.

Players: A pitch that hits the plate is considered a ball (A) unless the batter swings at the pitch (B).

Umpires: Be sure the play is completed and the ball is beyond the batter's reach before calling "Ball."

Reference: Rule 7, Sec. 7.

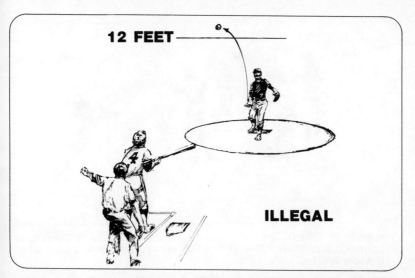

12 FEET

ILLEGAL

Players: An illegal pitch will be called at the time the pitch becomes illegal, but the ball remains in play until the pitch or play is completed.

Umpires: Call "Illegal Pitch" at the time of violation and signal "Delayed Dead Ball." Make the call loud enough for the batter or other players to hear. Signal "Delayed Dead Ball." When the ball is dead, call "Ball." (FP ONLY) Runners are also awarded one base for an illegal pitch.

Reference: Rule 7, Sec. 7b.

Players: (SP ONLY) When a pitch outside of the strike zone hits the batter, it is called a ball.

Umpires: Signal and call "Time." Then call "Ball." There are no base awards in Slow Pitch.

Reference: Rule 7, Sec. 7c.

Players: (SP ONLY) The ball must be returned directly to the pitcher following a pitch. (FP ONLY) The ball may be thrown to a base when runners are on.

Umpires: Signal and call "Time." Award an additional ball to the batter.

Reference: Rule 7, Sec. 7d; Rule 6, Sec. 3e.

Players: The pitcher must deliver the next pitch to the batter within 20 seconds of receiving the ball.

Umpires: Signal and call "Time" if a violation occurs. Award a ball to the batter and warn the pitcher.

Reference: Rule 7, Sec. 7e.

FAIR BALL

FAIR BALL

FAIR BALL

Players: Where the ball first hits the ground has no bearing upon whether it is fair or foul. A batted ball becomes fair or foul by its position when it is touched, when it settles, or when it passes first or third base.

Umpires: Delay your call until the ball is touched, settles, or goes beyond first or third base.

Reference: Rule 7, Sec. 8a and 9a.

Players: A batted ball is neither fair nor foul until it is touched, settles, or goes beyond first or third base.

Umpires: Delay your call until the ball is beyond first or third base, settles, or is touched. Judgment is made by the position of the ball at the time it is touched or goes beyond the base. Make the call from a position on the foul line.

Reference: Rule 7, Sec. 8a and 9a; Rule 1, Sec. 26 and 21.

Players: Any batted ball which hits first, second, or third base is a fair ball.

Umpires: Signal "Fair Ball." No verbal call is made.

Reference: Rule 7, Sec. 8c; Rule 1, Sec. 21.

Players: A ball that goes over the base or over fair ground when it bounds past first or third base is a fair ball.

Umpires: Signal "Fair Ball." No verbal call is made for any fair ball.

Reference: Rule 7, Sec. 8b; Rule 1, Sec. 21.

Players: A fly or bouncing ball is judged fair or foul by the position of the ball at the time it is touched.

Umpires: If foul, signal and call "Foul Ball." If fair, point towards the center of the diamond. No verbal call is made.

Reference: Rule 7, Sec. 8e; Rule 1, Sec. 21 and 26.

Players: A foul ball is a legally batted ball which touches the body or clothing of an umpire or player or is blocked while on or over foul ground.

Umpires: Signal and call "Foul Ball."

Reference: Rule 7, Sec. 9d.

Players: A batted ball leaving the playing field over fair ground is a fair ball, regardless of where it lands after leaving the park.
Umpires: Signal "Fair Ball." No verbal call is made. Signal and call "Home Run."
Reference: Rule 7, Sec. 8f; Rule 1, Sec. 21.

Players: A fly ball which hits the foul pole on a fly is a fair ball, even if it bounces to foul territory.
Umpires: Signal "Fair Ball." No verbal call is made. Signal and call "Home Run."
Reference: Rule 7, Sec. 8g; Rule 1, Sec. 21.

Players: When a batted ball bounds over foul territory, hits the bat a second time, and rolls into fair territory, it is considered a foul ball.

Umpires: Signal and call "Time." Then signal "Foul Ball" as soon as the ball becomes blocked. The batter is not called out for hitting the ball a second time with the bat. NOTE: If this was the third strike in Slow Pitch, the batter would be called out.

Reference: Rule 1, Sec. 26; Rule 7, Sec. 9d and 11 j (SP).

Players: If a fly foul ball goes above the batter's head and is caught, it is an out. If the ball does not go above the batter's head and is caught, it is a foul tip.

Umpires: Signal and call "Out." The ball remains in play.

Reference: Rule 7, Sec. 11c and 10; Rule 9, Sec. 2t.

Players: A trapped ball is not called a fly ball. A ball must be caught before hitting the ground or fence. A trapped ball is not considered to have been intentionally dropped.

Umpires: Signal and call "Safe" when the ball touches the ground or fence before the catch. Move to a position where you have a clear view of the trapped ball — do not run straight toward the ball.

Reference: Rule 7, Sec. 11e NOTE.

SAFE

OUT

Players: The batter is out when a fielder intentionally drops a fair fly ball including (FP and SP) a line drive or (FP ONLY) a bunt which can be caught by an infielder with ordinary effort with first, first and second, first and third, or first, second, and third bases occupied and with less than two outs. NOTE: This does not include a trapped ball or a ball that falls to the ground untouched or merely touched. It does include a ball that is guided to the ground with the glove and hand.

Umpires: Signal and call "Time." Then signal and call "Batter Out." Runners must return to the last base touched at the time of the pitch. Do not confuse this with the infield fly rule where the ball is alive, runners may advance at their own risk, and different runner situations are in force.

Reference: Rule 7, Sec. 11e; Rule 9, Sec. 1ac.

Players: When a runner interferes with a fielder attempting to field a batted ball, the runner is out whether or not the interference is intentional. If this interference, in the umpire's judgment, is an obvious attempt to prevent a double play, the immediate succeeding runner will be called out. No other runners may advance unless forced to do so by the batter-runner.

Umpires: Signal and call "Time — Interference." Then signal and call "Runner Out." Remember: a runner may not in any way impede, hinder, or confuse a fielder attempting to field a batted ball.

Reference: Rule 7, Sec. 11f and 4; Rule 8, Sec. 8j; Rule 1, Sec. 37; Rule 9, Sec. 1h.

Players: When a runner intentionally interferes with a fielder attempting to catch or throw a ball, the runner is out. If the runner has prevented a double play, the succeeding runner is also out.

Umpires: Signal and call "Time — Intentional Interference." Then signal and call "Runner Out" and "Batter-Runner Out." All other runners must return to the last base touched at the time of the interference.

Reference: Rule 7, Sec. 11f; Rule 8, Sec. 8j; Rule 1, Sec. 37; Rule 9, Sec. 1h.

Players: (FP ONLY) The batter is out, following a third strike, when the catcher catches the ball. The ball remains in play. Runners may advance.

Umpires: Signal and call "Strike Three." Do not call "Batter Out," since the catcher may drop the ball and the batter-runner could advance under certain conditions.

Reference: Rule 7, Sec. 11g; Rule 8, Sec. 2b.

Players: (FP ONLY) When first base is occupied and there are less than two outs, the batter is out following the third strike, whether the catcher catches the ball or not. NOTE: With two outs and first base occupied, the batter-runner may run following a dropped third strike by the catcher.

Umpires: Signal and call "Strike Three — Batter Out." The ball remains in play and runners may advance. With two outs, do not call "Batter Out."

Reference: Rule 7, Sec. 11h; Rule 8, Sec. 2b.

Players: (FP ONLY) The ball remains in play when the batter bunts a foul ball which is caught in the air. Runners may advance.

Umpires: Although the bunt is foul, the ball remains in play when it is a fly ball and is caught. On this play, delay your call until the catch is completed. Signal and call "Out." The ball is alive.

Reference: Rule 7, Sec. 11i.

Players: (FP ONLY) With two strikes, the batter is out if he or she bunts the ball foul.

Umpires: Delay your call until the ball is touched, comes to rest, or passes third base. Signal and call "Foul Ball." Then signal and call "Batter Out."

Reference: Rule 7, Sec. 11i; Rule 1, Sec. 11.

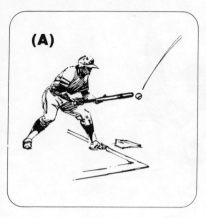

Players: (SP ONLY) The batter is out when he or she bunts or chops the ball downward (A and C). (A chopping motion is similar to chopping wood.) A check swing or short swing is not illegal (B and D).

Umpires: Signal and call "Time." Then signal and call "Batter Out." The ball is dead and all runners must return to the last base touched at the start of the pitch.

Reference: Rule 7, Sec. 11k.

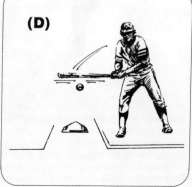

Players: The batter is out when discovered using an altered or illegal bat in the batter's box.

Umpires: When the batter enters the batter's box with an altered or illegal bat, signal and call "Time." Then signal and call "Batter Out" — illegal bat. If the bat is altered, remove the player from the game.

Reference: Rule 8, Sec. 7j.

Players: The on-deck batter is the offensive player who is next in line in the batting order. The on-deck batter must take a position within the lines of the on-deck circle nearest his or her team bench.

Umpires: If the on-deck batter does not take a position in the on-deck circle and delays the game, warn the manager to correct the problem.

Reference: Rule 7, Sec. 13a and b.

Players: (FP ONLY) When the on-deck batter interferes with the defensive fielder's opportunity to make a play on a runner, the runner closest to home plate at the time of the interference will be called out.

Umpires: When the interference occurs, signal and call "Time." Then signal and call "Runner Out" for the runner closest to home plate. The ball is dead. Inform the on-deck batter of the interference.

Reference: Rule 7, Sec. 13d.

Players: The on-deck batter may not interfere with a fielder attempting to catch a foul fly ball. The on-deck batter must vacate any area needed by a fielder who has a reasonable chance of making the catch.

Umpires: Signal and call "Time." Then signal and call "Batter Out" for interference. The ball is dead and the runners must return to the last base touched at the time of the pitch.

Reference: Rule 7, Sec. 13d and e, and Sec. 4.

Players: The on-deck batter may leave the circle to become the batter, to allow a defensive player the opportunity to field a ball, or to direct runners advancing from third base to home plate.

Umpires: The on-deck batter essentially has no safe place on the field. The on-deck batter may not interfere with any play, intentionally or unintentionally. During the play, be aware of the on-deck batter's position. If interference occurs at home plate when a defensive player has an opportunity to make a play on the runner, signal and call "Time." Then call "Runner Out" for the runner closest to home plate at the time of the interference.

Reference: Rule 7, Sec. 13c and d.

Section 4

Rule 8

Baserunning

ADVANCE

RETURN

Players: When returning to a base, the runner must tag each base in reverse order.

Umpires: The requirement to tag the bases in reverse order only applies when the ball is in play and the runner must return to a base, such as to tag up following a fly ball. No call is made until appealed by the defense, as with any other missed base. NOTE: If a runner missed a base when advancing, it is assumed (for purposes of returning and tagging in reverse) that the runner tagged that base. Just because the runner missed the base going forward, does not give him or her the right to miss the same base when returning.

Reference: Rule 8, Sec. 1a.

(A)

Players: A runner is entitled to hold a base until he or she has legally touched the next base or is forced to vacate it for a succeeding runner. A runner is forced to vacate the base when the batter-runner advances. The runner is not safe even while standing on the base if the fielder tags the runner before tagging the base (A and B).

Umpires: This situation can cause uncertainty for the players. Be clear and decisive in your call to avoid confusion. Signal and call "Out." Do not call "Time" until all play has been completed. NOTE: If the fielder tags first base before the runner, the force-out is eliminated and the runner does not have to leave the base in favor of the batter-runner (C).

Reference: Rule 8, Sec. 1b; Rule 1, Sec. 25; Rule 8, Sec. 7d.

(B)

(C)

OUT

SAFE

Players: Two runners may not occupy the same base at the same time. The runner who first legally occupied the base is entitled to it; the other runner may be tagged out with the ball.

Umpires: The trailing runner must be tagged while both runners are touching the same base. Signal and call "Safe" or "Out" for each runner. Any runner who leaves the base may be tagged out. The ball remains in play unless an umpire calls "Time."

Reference: Rule 8, Sec. 1e.

Players: When a base is dislodged, the dislodging has no effect upon the play (A).

Umpires: Determine your call as though the base was in place and by the timing of the tag (B). Signal and call "Safe."

Reference: Rule 8, Sec. 1c; Rule 1, Sec. 19.

Players: A fake tag is considered a form of obstructing a runner. A fielder without the ball may not fake a tag.

Umpires: Signal and call "Delayed Dead Ball — Obstruction." Award all runners the bases they would have reached had there been no obstruction. A warning should be given to both teams. The next fake tag warrants removal of the player from the game. A player may be removed from the game without warning if the umpire feels there is justification.

Reference: Rule 8, Sec. 5b (3).

Players: A runner may not run the bases in reverse order to confuse the fielders or to make a travesty of the game.

Umpires: Signal and call "Time." Then signal and call "Out." The ball is dead.

Reference: Rule 8, Sec. 1d.

(A)

Players: When a runner dislodges a base from its proper position (A) neither the runner or succeeding runners (B) in the same series of plays are compelled to follow a base unreasonably out of position.

Umpires: The runner should run reasonably close to the unmarked base path. If an appeal is made, signal and call "Safe" if the runner stepped where the base properly belongs.

Reference: Rule 8, Sec. 1c; Rule 1, Sec. 19.

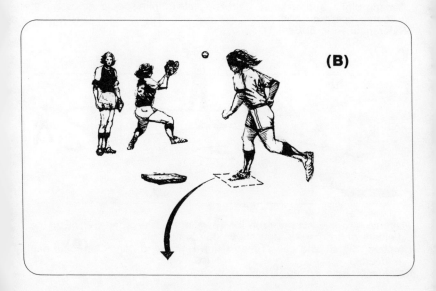

(B)

(A)

Players: When a preceding runner misses a base or fails to legally leave a base on a caught fly ball and is called out (A), it has no affect on the status of a succeeding runner who touches bases in proper order. However, if the preceding runner is the third out of the inning, no succeeding runner may score a run.

Umpires: Delay your call and observe the play. If a proper appeal is made, signal and make the call. The plate umpire should indicate to the scorekeeper and both teams the number of runs scoring (B).

Reference: Rule 8, Sec. 1f.

(B)

Players: No runner may return to tag a missed base after a following runner has scored.

Umpires: If the first runner returns to tag the missed base, it is ignored. Upon a proper appeal, the first runner would be called out.

Reference: Rule 8, Sec. 1g.

Players: When a live ball is unintentionally carried by a fielder from playable territory into dead ball territory, the ball becomes dead.
Umpires: Signal and call "Time." Award all baserunners one (1) base beyond the last base touched at the time the fielder entered dead ball territory. A fielder carrying a live ball into the dugout or team area to tag a player is considered to have unintentionally carried it there.
Reference: Rule 8, Sec. 5k.

Players: A runner who has *not* advanced to the next base may return to the previous base to tag the base during a dead ball.
Umpires: Do not award bases until the runner has returned to the original base. NOTE: If an award is made and the runner does not return, the defensive team can make an appeal and the runner would be called out.
Reference: Rule 8, Sec. 1g.

(A)

Players: A runner who enters the dugout or bench area may not return to tag a missed base (A and B).

Umpires: Ignore any such tagging. Do not announce to either team that you are ignoring the return to the base, since it would give away the appeal play. If an appeal is made, signal and call "Runner Out."

Reference: Rule 8, Sec. 1h.

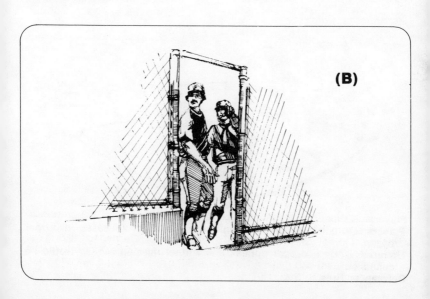

(B)

Players: A runner who has advanced to a base beyond a missed base, or beyond the base he or she left illegally, may not return to tag the missed base during a dead ball, even after the ball becomes alive.

Umpires: If a runner returns to tag the missed base during a dead ball, it is ignored. Do not announce to either team that you are ignoring the return to the base, since it would give away the appeal play. Upon a proper appeal, the runner would be called out.

Reference: Rule 8, Sec. 1g.

Players: On a home run, the runners must touch all bases in proper order.

Umpires: Upon a proper appeal, any runner missing a base would be called out.

Reference: Rule 8, Sec. 1k.

Players: After a walk is issued, all runners must touch all bases in proper order. Failure to touch each base would allow the defensive team to make an appeal and no runs would score.

Umpires: Be alert to this play, especially near the end of the game. The excitement of the teams should not override your duty and the application of the rule. Should a proper appeal be made before the defensive team leaves fair territory, the batter-runner or other runner who failed to touch a base would be called out. No runs would score and the game would not be over.

Reference: Rule 8, Sec. 1i.

Players: When a fair batted ball strikes the umpire or a baserunner after having passed an infielder, other than the pitcher, or having been touched by an infielder including the pitcher, the ball remains in play.

Umpires: Allow all play to continue with runners advancing at their own risk.

Reference: Rule 8, Sec. 3e.

VIOLATION

Players: A runner must touch all awarded bases in proper order. NOTE: If a base is missed on the award (during the dead ball) and the runner advances to and touches the next base, he or she cannot return to touch the missed base and could be called out if an appeal is made.

Umpires: Announce awarded bases separately. Upon a proper appeal, any runner missing an awarded base would be called out if the base or the runner missing the base is tagged.

Reference: Rule 8, Sec. 1k.

Players: (FP ONLY) The batter-runner may advance following a third strike (called or swinging) if the catcher does not catch the ball. NOTE: If there are less than two outs and first base is occupied, the batter is out whether the pitch is caught or not.

Umpires: Signal and call "Strike Three." Do not signal and call "Batter Out" until the play has been completed. If the batter is allowed to advance, do not call "Out" until the batter is tagged or forced out.

Reference: Rule 8, Sec. 2b.

Players: (FP ONLY) A ball hitting the ground during a third strike is not considered a catch. The batter may advance and can only be put out when tagged or when first base is tagged before the batter-runner reaches it.

Umpires: Signal and call "Strike Three." No other signal or call is made until the batter-runner is safe or out.

Reference: Rule 8, Sec. 2b.

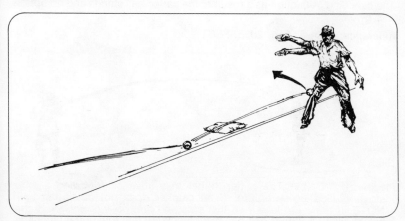

Players: When a fair ball hits an umpire in foul territory, the ball remains in play and runners may advance.

Umpires: Signal and call "Fair Ball."

Reference: Rule 8, Sec. 2c and 3e.

Players: The batter becomes a batter-baserunner when the catcher or any other fielder obstructs the batter or prevents him or her from striking at a pitched ball.

Umpires: Signal "Delayed Dead Ball." Then signal and call "Time." The ball is dead and the batter is awarded first base. Baserunners may not advance unless forced to do so by the batter-runner. The manager of the offensive team has the option of taking the award for catcher obstruction or taking the result of the play. However, if the batter hits the ball and reaches first base safely and if all other runners have advanced at least one base on the batted ball, the catcher obstruction is canceled. All action as a result of the batted ball stands and no option is given.

Reference: Rule 8, Sec. 2d EFFECT.

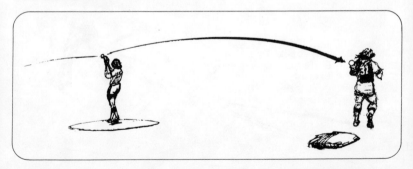

Players: When a batted ball has been fielded or has touched an infielder or pitcher, it is incidental and ignored if the ball touches the runner.
Umpires: No call is made. If the players appear confused, signal and call "Safe."
Reference: Rule 8, Sec. 3e.

Players: (FP ONLY) When the pitch hits the batter, the ball is dead and the batter is awarded first base. The hands are not considered part of the bat. It does not matter if the ball touched the ground before hitting the batter. The batter must make an attempt to avoid being hit by the pitch. If the batter doesn't, the umpire calls ball or strike.
Umpires: Signal and call "Time."
Reference: Rule 8, Sec. 2f; Rule 7, Sec. 6e; Rule 9, Sec. 1e.

Players: A runner may leave the base after a fly ball has been touched. The runner need not stay on the base until the catch is completed. The runner need not be on the base at the time the ball is caught, but must retouch the base before advancing.
Umpires: No signal or call is required until an appeal is made. Should the runner leave too soon and fail to return for a tag up, keep this information to yourself. If a proper appeal is made, then the runner should be called out.
Reference: Rule 8, Sec. 3d.

Players: (FP ONLY) The batter is awarded one base when a pitched ball, which is not struck at or called a strike, touches any part of the batter's body or clothing while he or she is in the batter's box. It does not matter if the ball strikes the ground before hitting the batter, but the batter must make an effort to avoid being hit.

Umpires: The ball is dead. Signal and call "Time" and award the batter one base. The batter is allowed whatever time is necessary to recover from any injury. Other runners may advance if forced to do so by the batter-runner. NOTE: If the batter makes no attempt to avoid being hit, the ball is dead, but no award is made. Only a ball is called on the batter.

Reference: Rule 8, Sec. 2f; Rule 9, Sec. 1e.

Players: A batter-runner may overrun (or slide) first base and return directly to the base without liability of being tagged out. The runner may choose to turn in either direction. The runner may be tagged out when there is an attempt or movement toward second base. Simply turning is not an attempt to go to second base.

Umpires: No signal or call is required until a tag is applied. Whether a runner simply turns or attempts to advance toward second base is an umpire's judgment.

Reference: Rule 8, Sec. 4b; Rule 1, Sec. 44.

Players: Obstruction occurs when a fielder intentionally or unintentionally impedes the progress of a runner. If the runner is not being played upon, the ball remains in play.

Umpires: Signal and call "Delayed Dead Ball — Obstruction" loud enough so the immediate players can hear. When all play has been completed, award the bases that the runner would have reached had there been no obstruction. If the runner has gone beyond that base which, in your mind, he or she would have reached had there been no obstruction, the runner may be tagged out.

Reference: Rule 8, Sec. 5b (2) and (3); Rule 1, Sec. 41.

Players: If a runner is pushed off base during a play, it is considered obstruction. The ball becomes dead and the obstructed runner is awarded one base beyond the last base legally touched.

Umpires: Signal and call "Time — Obstruction." Award at least one base beyond the last base touched. Any preceding runner forced to advance by the award to the obstructed runner will also be advanced one base.

Reference: Rule 8, Sec. 5b (1); Rule 1, Sec. 41.

RUNDOWN

Players: Blocking a runner's path to a base is obstruction. If the runner is being played upon, the ball is dead and at least one base is awarded.
Umpires: Signal and call "Time — Obstruction" and award the runner at least one base beyond the last base touched. The base the runner is going toward does not matter. If a runner is going back to a base, the award should be forward to the base beyond the last one touched.
Reference: Rule 8, Sec. 5b (1); Rule 1, Sec. 41.

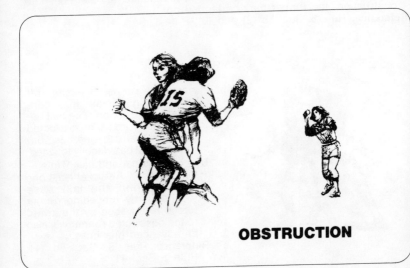

OBSTRUCTION

Players: When a defensive player with the ball (A) is between the runner and the next base, and the runner remains on his or her feet and deliberately collides into the fielder (B), the runner is out and the ball is dead (C).

Umpires: Usually two steps constitute more than adequate reaction time for a runner to decide whether to slide or return to the previous base. If the runner collides into the fielder, signal and call "Time." Then signal and call "Runner Out." If the collision is flagrant, remove the runner from the game.

Reference: Rule 8, Sec. 5c.

Players: (FP ONLY) When a pitch goes under, over, through, or lodges in the backstop, fence, or out-of-play area, each runner is awarded one base. The batter may advance to first base only if the pitch was ball four.

Umpires: Signal and call "Time" and award the bases.

Reference: Rule 8, Sec. 5d.

LEGAL

NO CONTACT

Players: A fielder may not contact or catch a batted or thrown ball with a cap, glove, mask, or any part of the uniform detached from its proper place.

ILLEGAL

Umpires: Simply throwing a cap or glove at the ball is not illegal. *It is illegal only when contact is made with the ball.* If a thrown ball, all runners may advance two bases. If a batted ball, all runners are entitled to advance three bases unless the ball would have been a fair home run out of the playing field. In this case, a home run is awarded. NOTE: After play has ceased or the ball has gone out of play, signal and call "Time" and make the awards as necessary. The ball is alive if contact is made and runners can advance at their own risk beyond those bases awarded.

Reference: Rule 8, Sec. 5g.

Players: When a ball is thrown out of play, each runner is awarded two bases from the last base touched at the time the ball is released. The base the runner is going to has no affect on the award. The award always advances the runners.

Umpires: Signal and call "Time" and award two bases to all runners. The award is based on the position of the runners at the start of the pitch (when the first throw was made by an infielder) or by the position of the runners and the last base they had touched (when the throw was released by an outfielder or a succeeding play by an infielder was made).

Reference: Rule 8, Sec. 5h; Rule 9, Sec. 1z; Rule 1, Sec. 10.

OUT OF PLAY LINE

Players: When a fielder loses possession of the ball, such as on an attempted tag, and it goes out of play, each runner is awarded one base beyond the last base touched at the time the ball entered the out-of-play area. The runner sliding into third base would have reached this base before the ball went out of play, and would therefore be awarded home plate.

Umpires: It is not considered a throw when the fielder loses possession of the ball. Awards are judged by the positions of the runners at the time the ball leaves the playing field. Signal and call "Time" and award one base to each runner.

Reference: Rule 8, Sec. 5h; Rule 9, Sec. 1z; Rule 1, Sec. 10.

Players: When a fair ball bounds or rolls into a stand, or goes over, under, or through a fence, the ball is dead. All runners including the batter-runner are awarded two bases beyond the last base touched at the start of the pitch.

Umpires: Move to a position where you can see the ball going under, over, or through the fence. Signal and call "Two Bases." All runners including the batter-runner are awarded two bases beyond the last base touched at the start of the pitch.

Reference: Rule 8, Sec. 5j.

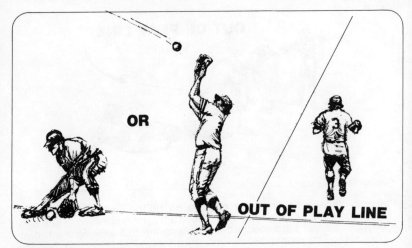

OR

OUT OF PLAY LINE

Players: When a live ball is intentionally carried from playable territory into dead ball territory, the ball becomes dead.

Umpires: Signal and call "Time." Award all baserunners two bases beyond the last base touched at the time the ball entered dead ball territory.

Reference: Rule 8, Sec. 5k.

OUT OF PLAY LINE

Players: If a fly ball is legally caught within the playing field and is unintentionally carried to the out-of-play area, the batter is out and each runner is awarded one base.

Umpires: If the catch is completed before the player or ball touches anything outside the playing area, signal and call "Out." When the ball leaves the playing area, signal and call "Time." Award each runner one base beyond the one held at the time of the pitch.

Reference: Rule 8, Sec. 5k; Rule 7, Sec. 11c.

Players: When a fair deflected ball goes over the fence on the fly, it is a home run. When a fair deflected ball bounces before going over the fence, it is a double.

Umpires: Move to a position where you can see the ball going over the fence. Signal either a home run or a double and call "Time." If the batted ball is a double, all runners including the batter-runner are awarded two bases beyond the last base touched at the start of the pitch. NOTE: If a fielder makes a legal catch and falls over the fence out of play, it is a good catch. Signal "Out" and "Time" and award all runners one base beyond the last base touched at the start of the pitch.

Reference: Rule 8, Sec. 5j and k.

Players: To complete a force out, a fielder may legally tag a base with any part of the body or glove before the runner touches the base, even if the tag is made without the ball in that hand.

Umpires: Signal and call "Out."

Reference: Rule 8, Sec. 7d.

Players: (FP ONLY) When the umpire interferes with the catcher's throw, the runner must return to the last base touched at the time of the interference if the runner is safe.

Umpires: Call "Umpire Interference" loud enough for the catcher and batter to hear. If the runner is tagged out, ignore the interference. If the runner is safe, he or she must return to the last base touched at the time of the interference.

Reference: Rule 8, Sec. 6d (FP ONLY).

Players: When a batter-runner enters the dugout prior to going to first base after a fair ball is hit, after four balls are called, or (FP ONLY) after a dropped third strike, the batter-runner is out.

Umpires: When the batter-runner advances to the team area rather than going directly to first base, signal and call "Batter-Runner Out." The ball remains in play.

Reference: Rule 8, Sec. 7f.

Players: (SP ONLY) Under no conditions except an awarded base is a runner allowed to advance on a pitch that is not batted. Stealing is not permitted.

Umpires: Signal and call "Time." The runner must return to the last base touched at the start of the pitch. There is no penalty when a runner leaves the base after the ball reaches home plate.

Reference: Rule 8, Sec. 6h; Rule 1, Sec. 52; Rule 9, Sec. 1x.

Players: When the batter-runner interferes with a play at home plate, the batter and the runner are both out. The ball is dead and a double play is called.

Umpires: This is a deliberate attempt to prevent the play at home plate. A double play penalty is imposed. Signal and call "Time." Then signal and call "Runner Out" and Batter Out."

Reference: Rule 8, Sec. 7i.

Players: When the batter runs outside of the 3-foot line the last half distance to first base and interferes with the play, the batter-runner is out. NOTE: The batter-runner may run outside the 3-foot line to avoid a fielder attempting to field a batted ball.

Umpires: Signal and call "Time." Then signal and call "Batter-Runner Out." The other runners must return to the last base touched. The ball need not hit the runner for interference to be called. Interference is when the runner impedes, hinders, or confuses the fielders attempting the play.

Reference: Rule 8, Sec. 7g; Rule 1, Sec. 37.

Players: A runner may use any route to get to a base until there is an attempted tag. When attempting to avoid a tag, a runner may not run more than three feet from a direct line to the base.

Umpires: The length of the fielder's arm is considered to be three feet. If the fielder's body is in the runner's base path and the runner goes around the tag, signal and call "Out" — runner out of the base line. The ball remains in play.

Reference: Rule 8, Sec. 8a and 9b.

Players: When a runner passes a preceding runner before either one is tagged out, the passing runner is out.

Umpires: As soon as the trailing runner passes the preceding runner, signal and call "Runner Out" for passing a runner. Point to the runner who is out. The ball remains in play.

Reference: Rule 8, Sec. 8e.

Players: When the batter-runner moves back toward home plate to avoid or delay a tag by a fielder, the batter-runner is out and the ball is dead. All runners must return to the last base touched.

Umpires: Signal and call "Time." Then signal and call "Batter Out."

Reference: Rule 8, Sec. 8q.

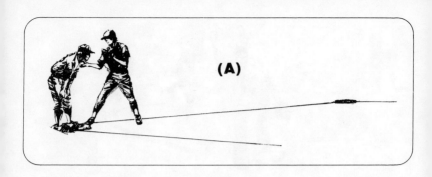

Players: While the ball is in play, an appeal play may be made by tagging the runner who missed the base (A), or by tagging the base that was missed (B).

Umpires: Be sure you know the reasons for any appeal before announcing a decision. If you do not have the information, you may ask the players for this.

Reference: Rule 8, Sec. 8f and g; Rule 1, Sec. 2; Rule 9, Sec. 2b.

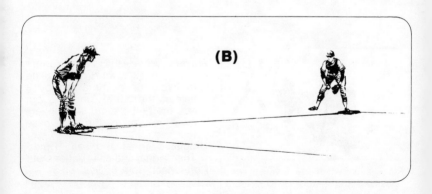

Players: When a baserunner intentionally interferes with a fielder attempting to field a batted ball or intentionally interferes with a thrown ball, the runner is out. If the interference is an attempt to prevent a double play, the succeeding runner is also out.

Umpires: Signal and call "Time — Interference." Signal and call both runners "Out." The ball is dead and other runners must return to the last base touched.

Reference: Rule 8, Sec. 8j; Rule 9, Sec. 1h and k.

Players: When a fair ball strikes a runner on fair ground and has not passed an infielder or touched a player, the runner is out. NOTE: A ball touching a runner in foul territory is a foul ball.

Umpires: Signal and call "Time." Then signal and call "Runner Out." Award the batter-runner first base and a base hit. All runners not forced to advance by the batter-runner must return to the last base touched at the time the ball hit the runner.

Reference: Rule 8, Sec. 8k, 2f, and 6c.

Players: When anyone other than another baserunner physically assists a baserunner while the ball is in play, the runner is out.

Umpires: Signal and call "Time." Then signal and call "Runner Out" for the assistance. The ball is dead. All other runners must return to the last base touched at the time of the illegal action.

Reference: Rule 8, Sec. 8n and Rule 8, Sec. 8j-s.

Players: When a runner, after being declared out or after scoring, interferes with a fielder's opportunity to make another play, the runner closest to home plate will be declared out.

Umpires: Because the runner causing the interference is already out, the runner closest to home plate will be called out. Signal and call "Time — Interference." Then signal and call "Runner Out" for the runner closest to home plate. (This could be the batter-runner.) The ball is dead. NOTE: If a runner scores before the interference, the run would count and the next closest runner to home plate would be called out.

Reference: Rule 8, Sec. 8s; Rule 1, Sec. 37; Rule 9, Sec. 1h.

Players: (FP ONLY) When the pitcher has the ball in the 8-foot radius, all runners must immediately proceed to the next base or return to the last base touched. Failure to do so will result in the runner being called out.

Umpires: Observe the runner. If he or she does not move one way or the other once the pitcher has the ball in the 8-foot radius, signal and call "Time." Then signal and call "Runner Out." The ball is dead.

Reference: Rule 8, Sec. 8t (FP ONLY) (1).

Players: A runner who has legally started to advance cannot be stopped by the pitcher receiving the ball while on the pitching plate or within the circle.

Umpires: Do not call "Time" while a play is in progress. Allow the play to be completed.

Reference: Rule 8, Sec. 9i.

Players: Baserunners may leave their bases on appeal plays when the ball leaves the 8-foot (2.44 m) circle around the pitcher's plate, when the ball leaves the pitcher's possession, or when the pitcher makes a motion indicating a play or fake throw.

Umpires: If a runner leaves too soon, signal and call "Time." Then signal and call "Out" for leaving too soon.

Reference: Rule 8, Sec. 8f-i (3).

Players: (FP ONLY) Runners must maintain contact with the base until the ball leaves the pitcher's hand. (SP ONLY) Runners must maintain contact with the base until the ball is hit or reaches home plate.
Umpires: If the runner leaves too soon, signal and call "Time — No Pitch." Then signal and call "Runner Out" for leaving to soon.
Reference: Rule 8, Sec. 8t and u; Rule 9, Sec. 1g.

Players: (SP ONLY) Runners may leave their bases when the ball reaches home plate or is batted.

Umpires: If the runner leaves too soon, signal and call "Time — No Pitch." Then signal and call "Runner Out" for leaving too soon.

Reference: Rule 8, Sec. 8u.

(A)

(B)

Players: (FP ONLY) When four balls or a dropped third strike is called, runners may advance just as with a batted ball. The batter-runner may continue past first base and is entitled to run toward second base, as long as he or she does not stop at first base before continuing to second base.

Umpires: When the pitcher holds the ball within the 8-foot radius of the pitching plate, a runner may run across the base (A), but may not walk across it (B). Running across is defined as continuation. If the runner stops after rounding first base, then he or she must immediately proceed to second base or return to first base. If the runner does not comply or steps off first base after stopping while the pitcher has the ball in the 8-foot radius, signal and call "Runner Out."

Reference: Rule 8, Sec. 8t NOTE and 2b (FP ONLY).

Section 5

Rules 9 and 10

Dead Ball, Ball in Play, and Umpires

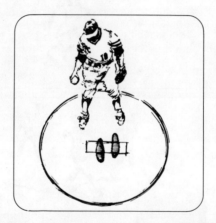

Players: If the pitcher takes a position on the pitching plate and requests an appeal, he or she must step backward off the pitching plate before throwing to a base.

Umpires: Signal and call "Play Ball" when the appeal is requested. If the pitcher steps backward off the plate, the ball remains in play for the appeal. If the pitcher throws from the pitching plate, or steps toward the base from the pitching plate, it is an illegal pitch and the appeal is cancelled. (FP ONLY) Runners advance on base. (SP ONLY) Runners must return to the last base touched.

Reference: Rule 9, Sec. 2b; Rule 6 (FP and SP), Sec. 8.

(A)

Players: When a fair infield fly ball strikes a runner, the ball is dead. If the runner is not touching a base when hit with the ball, the runner is out (A). If the runner is touching a base when hit with the ball, the runner is safe (B). The infield fly rule is not affected by the runner being hit with the ball — the batter is automatically out.

Umpires: Signal and call "Infield Fly" if fair. Then signal and call "Batter Out." When the ball strikes the runner, signal and call "Time." If the runner is off the base when hit, signal and call "Runner Out." If the runner is on the base when hit, signal and call "Runner Safe." Do not be in a hurry to make your call.

Reference: Rule 9, Sec. 1h (3); Rule 1, Sec. 35; Rule 8, Sec. 8k.

(B)

Players: (SP ONLY) No runners may advance when the ball goes into the outfield as a result of the catcher overthrowing the pitcher following a pitch.

Umpires: The ball is dead when not hit by the batter and is not put into play again until the pitcher steps on the pitching plate ready to pitch. All runners must return to the last base touched at the start of the pitch.

Reference: Rule 9, Sec. 1x (SP ONLY).

Players: If a batter-runner becomes injured after hitting a home run out of the ball park and cannot continue running, a substitute runner may complete the play.

Umpires: If an accident prevents a runner from proceeding to an awarded base, a substitute runner may complete the play.

Reference: Rule 9, Sec. 1j.

PLAY BALL

Players: When time has been called, the pitcher may initiate an appeal play by holding the ball and standing off the pitching plate within the 8-foot radius and requesting the appeal. Only after the umpire calls "Play Ball" can the appeal be completed.

Umpires: When an appeal is requested during a dead ball, signal and call "Play Ball" even if the batter is not in the batter's box. The pitcher must be within the 8-foot radius of the pitching plate but does not have to be on it.

Reference: Rule 9, Sec. 2b; Rule 1, Sec. 2.

Players: a pitched ball which bounces to home plate and is hit by the batter is a legally batted ball.

Umpires: Delay your call until the ball is beyond the batter's reach. *If* the ball is hit, signal "Fair Ball" or signal and call "Foul Ball."

Reference: Rule 9, Sec. 2r; Rule 7, Sec. 7; Rule 10, Sec. e and f.

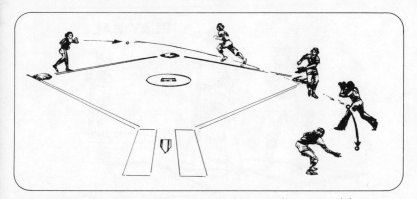

Players: When a thrown ball strikes a photographer, groundskeeper, or police officer assigned to the game, the ball remains in play. Runners may advance.

Umpires: It is not considered interference when an assigned photographer is hit with a thrown ball. Allow all play to continue with runners advancing at their own risk.

Reference: Rule 9, Sec. 2s.

Players: When a thrown ball strikes an umpire, the ball remains in play. Runners may advance.

Umpires: It is not considered interference when an umpire is hit with a thrown ball. Allow all play to continue with runners advancing at their own risk.

Reference: Rule 9, Sec. 2w.

Players: No player, coach, or manager can request the umpire to call "Time" even if a player is injured.

Umpires: Delay your call until no further play is possible. Signal and call "Time." NOTE: The ball does not become dead when a player is injured during a batted or thrown ball.

Reference: Rule 10, Sec. 8g.

Umpire Signal Chart

GAME SIGNALS

Safe: Extend arms, palms down. Make verbal call.

Out: Hold right fist above head. If plate umpire, hold mask in left hand. Make verbal call.

Strike: Raise right hand up and then extend to side indicating the number of strikes with the fingers. Make verbal call.

Fair Ball: Make a pumping motion toward the infield. *No verbal call.* Keep mask in opposite hand.

Foul Ball: Point away from the playing field with both arms. Make verbal call.

Time Out: Extend both arms above the head. Make verbal call.

Play Ball: Motion pitcher to deliver ball. Make verbal call.

Play Ball: Motion to pitcher in 8-foot radius for an appeal play. Make verbal call.

Delayed Dead Ball: Extend left arm horizontally.

119

Trapped Ball: Extend both arms horizontally, similar to the safe signal.

Foul Tip: Touch fingers of both hands together to indicate that the bat tipped the ball.

Count: Use the left hand for "Balls" and the right hand for "Strikes," using the fingers to indicate the number.

Infield Fly: Extend right hand above the head. Make verbal call. If near foul line, call "Infield Fly" if fair.

Double: Raise one arm above the head indicating with two fingers the number of bases awarded. Make verbal call.

Home Run: Raise one arm above the head with a closed fist and make a clockwise circling motion.

No Pitch: Raise one hand with the palm facing the pitcher. No verbal call necessary unless the pitcher pitches while signal is given.

CREW SIGNALS

Plate Umpire: Request help on a half or check swing by removing mask and pointing to field umpire.

Field Umpire: Indicate *yes* it is a strike by giving a definite strike signal.

Field Umpire: Indicate *no* the batter did not swing by giving a safe signal.

Umpires: Indicate an infield fly situation by crossing right hand over left chest.

Umpires: Indicate an infield fly situation is now off by brushing left arm downward with right hand.

Umpires: Request the number of outs in the inning by clenching right fist and tapping on the right thigh.

Umpires: Indicate the number of outs by giving count on fingers on right thigh.

Umpires: Request the ball and strike count by holding open hands on the chest.

Umpires: Respond to request for the ball and strike count by holding fingers above head to indicate the number

INDEX

INDEX (continued)

INDEX (continued)